MAYA A_____ Louis, Missouri. A_____ arents' marriage she a___ h__ ____ l brot__ ley went to live with the_r ____m___ _r, whos_ ___ral store was the centre o_ ___ or __e Black community in Stamps, Arkansas. At eight Maya was raped by her mother's boyfriend and for the next five years she became mute. In her teens she and Bailey moved to California to live with their mother, and at sixteen, having graduated from school, Maya gave birth to her son, Guy.

In the years that followed she has been waitress, singer, actress, dancer, Black activist, editor, as well as mother. She has had, as she describes it "a roller coaster life ... there has been this disappointment and that satisfaction, and then it begins all over again". In her twenties she toured Europe and Africa in *Porgy and Bess*. Moving to New York, she joined the Harlem Writers Guild and continued to earn her living as a night-club singer and performer in Genet's *The Blacks*. She became involved in Black struggles in the 1960s and then spent several years in Ghana as editor of *African Review*. She has now returned to the South and teaches American Studies at Wake Forest University in North Carolina.

In addition to her earlier collection of poems, *And Still I Rise*, and *Just Give Me a Cool Drink of Water 'fore I Diiie*, Virago publish Maya Angelou's remarkable volumes of autobiography, *I Know Why the Caged Bird Sings, Gather Together in My Name, Singin' and Swingin' and Gettin' Merry Like Christmas, The Heart of a Woman,* and *All God's Children Need Travelling Shoes*, as well as her poetic *Now Sheba Sings the Song*, with drawings by Tom Feelings.

Just Give Me a Cool Drink of Water 'fore I Diiie

THE POETRY OF

Maya Angelou

Published by VIRAGO PRESS Limited 1988
Centro House, 20–23 Mandela Street, Camden Town,
London NW1 0HQ.

British Library Cataloguing in Publication Data

Angelou, Maya
  Just give me a cool drink of water 'fore
  I diiie.
  I. Title
  811'.54   PS3551.N464
  ISBN 0-86068-264-1

Printed in Great Britain by Cox & Wyman Ltd., Reading, Berks.

This Virago edition, *Just Give Me a Cool Drink of Water 'fore
I Diiie*, is made up of two of Maya Angelou's collections of
poetry, previously available only in the USA and Canada: *Just
Give Me a Cool Drink of Water 'fore I Diiie* (1971) and *Oh Pray
My Wings Are Gonna Fit Me Well* (1975) which were published
by Random House, Inc., New York, and Random House of
Canada Limited, Toronto.

CONTENTS

JUST GIVE ME A COOL DRINK OF WATER 'FORE I DIIIE

Part One
Where Love Is a Scream of Anguish

Part Two
Just Before the World Ends

OH PRAY MY WINGS ARE GONNA FIT ME WELL

Part One

Part Two

Part Three

Part Four

Part Five

To AMBER SAM

and the ZORRO MAN

Where Love Is a Scream of Anguish

They Went Home

They went home and told their wives,
    that never once in all their lives,
    had they known a girl like me,
But . . . They went home.

They said my house was licking clean,
    no word I spoke was ever mean,
    I had an air of mystery,
But . . . They went home.

My praises were on all men's lips,
    they liked my smile, my wit, my hips,
    they'd spend one night, or two or three.
But . . .

The Gamut

Soft you day, be velvet soft,
    My true love approaches,
Look you bright, you dusty sun,
    Array your golden coaches.

    Soft you wind, be soft as silk
My true love is speaking.
    Hold you birds, your silver throats,
His golden voice I'm seeking.

Come you death, in haste, do come
    My shroud of black be weaving,
Quiet my heart, be deathly quiet,
    My true love is leaving.

A Zorro Man

Here
in the wombed room
silk purple drapes
flash a light as subtle
as your hands before
love-making

Here
in the covered lens
I catch a
clitoral image of
your general inhabitation
long and like a
late dawn in winter

Here
this clean mirror
traps me unwilling
in a gone time
when I was love
and you were booted and brave
and trembling for me.

To a Man

My man is
Black Golden Amber
Changing.
Warm mouths of Brandy Fine
Cautious sunlight on a patterned rug
Coughing laughter, rocked on a whorl of French tobacco
Graceful turns on woolen stilts
Secretive?
A cat's eye.
Southern. Plump and tender with navy bean sullenness
And did I say "Tender"?
The gentleness
A big cat stalks through stubborn bush
And did I mention "Amber"?
The heatless fire consuming itself.
Again. Anew. Into ever neverlessness.
My man is Amber
Changing
Always into itself
New. Now New.
Still itself.
Still.

Late October

Carefully
the leaves of autumn
sprinkle down the tinny
sound of little dyings
and skies sated
of ruddy sunsets
of roseate dawns
roil ceaselessly in
cobweb greys and turn
to black
for comfort.

Only lovers
see the fall
a signal end to endings
a gruffish gesture alerting
those who will not be alarmed
that we begin to stop
in order simply
to begin
again.

No Loser, No Weeper

"I hate to lose something,"
    then she bent her head
"even a dime, I wish I was dead.
I can't explain it. No more to be said.
Cept I hate to lose something."

"I lost a doll once and cried for a week.
She could open her eyes, and do all but speak.
I believe she was took, by some doll-snatching-sneak
I tell you, I hate to lose something."

"A watch of mine once, got up and walked away.
It had twelve numbers on it and for the time of day.
I'll never forget it and all I can say
Is I really hate to lose something."

"Now if I felt that way bout a watch and a toy,
What you think I feel bout my lover-boy?
I ain't threatening you madam, but he is my evening's joy.
And I mean I really hate to lose something."

When You Come to Me

When you come to me, unbidden,
Beckoning me
   To long-ago rooms,
Where memories lie.

   Offering me, as to a child, an attic,
Gatherings of days too few.
   Baubles of stolen kisses.
Trinkets of borrowed loves.
   Trunks of secret words,

   I CRY.

Remembering

Soft grey ghosts crawl up my sleeve
to peer into my eyes
while I within deny their threats
and answer them with lies.

Mushlike memories perform
a ritual on my lips
I lie in stolid hopelessness
and they lay my soul in strips.

In a Time

In a time of secret wooing
Today prepares tomorrow's ruin
Left knows not what right is doing
My heart is torn asunder.

In a time of furtive sighs
Sweet hellos and sad goodbyes
Half-truths told and entire lies
My conscience echoes thunder

In a time when kingdoms come
Joy is brief as summer's fun
Happiness, its race has run
Then pain stalks in to plunder.

Tears

Tears
The crystal rags
Viscous tatters
of a worn-through soul

Moans
Deep swan song
Blue farewell
of a dying dream.

The Detached

We die,
Welcoming Bluebeards to our darkening closets,
Stranglers to our outstretched necks.
> Stranglers, who neither care nor
> care to know that
> DEATH IS INTERNAL.

We pray,
Savoring sweet the teethed lies,
Bellying the grounds before alien gods
> Gods, who neither know nor
> wish to know that
> HELL IS INTERNAL.

We love,
Rubbing the nakednesses with gloved hands
Inverting our mouths in tongued kisses,
> Kisses that neither touch nor
> care to touch if
> LOVE IS INTERNAL.

To a Husband

Your voice at times a fist
    Tight in your throat
Jabs ceaselessly at phantoms
    In the room,
Your hand a carved and
    skimming boat
Goes down the Nile
    To point out Pharoah's tomb.

You're Africa to me
    At brightest dawn.
The Congo's green and
    Copper's brackish hue,
A continent to build
    With Black Man's brawn.
I sit at home and see it all
    Through you.

Accident

tonight
>when you spread your pallet
of magic,
>I escaped.
sitting apart,
>I saw you grim and unkempt.
Your vulgar-ness
>not of living
your demands
>not from need.

tonight
>as you sprinkled your brain-dust
of rainbows,
>I had no eyes.
Seeing all
I saw the colors fade
and change.
>The blood, red dulled
through the dyes,
and the naked
Black-White truth.

Let's Majeste

I sit a throne upon the times
when Kings are rare and
Consorts
slide into the grease of scullery maids.

So gaily wave a crown of light
(astride the royal chair) that blinds
the commoners who genuflect and cross their fingers.

The years will lie beside me
on the queenly bed.
And coupled we'll await
the ages' dust to cake my lids again.

And when the rousing kiss is given,
why must it always be a fairy, and
only just a Prince?

After

No sound falls
from the moaning sky
No scowl wrinkles
the evening pool
 The stars lean down
 A stony brilliance
 While birds fly

The market leers
its empty shelves
Streets bare bosoms
to scanty cars
 This bed yawns
 beneath the weight
 of our absent selves.

The Mothering Blackness

She came home running
    back to the mothering blackness
    deep in the smothering blackness
white tears icicle gold plains of her face
    She came home running

She came down creeping
    here to the black arms waiting
    now to the warm heart waiting
rime of alien dreams befrost her rich brown face
    She came down creeping

She came home blameless
    black yet as Hagar's daughter
    tall as was Sheba's daughter
threats of northern winds die on the desert's face
    She came home blameless

On Diverse Deviations

When love is a shimmering curtain
Before a door of chance
That leads to a world in question
Wherein the macabrous dance
Of bones that rattle in silence
Of blinded eyes and rolls
Of thick lips thin, denying
A thousand powdered moles,
Where touch to touch is feel
And life a weary whore
    I would be carried off, not gently
    To a shore,
    Where love is the scream of anguish
    And no curtain drapes the door.

Mourning Grace

If today, I follow death
go down its trackless wastes,
salt my tongue on hardened tears
for my precious dear times waste
race
along that promised cave in a headlong
deadlong
haste,
Will you
have
the
grace
to mourn for
me?

How I Can Lie to You

now thread my voice
with lies
of lightness
force within
my mirror eyes
the cold disguise
of sad and wise
decisions.

Sounds Like Pearls

Sounds
    Like pearls
Roll off your tongue
    To grace this eager ebon ear.

Doubt and fear,
    Ungainly things,
With blushings
    Disappear.

Just Before the World Ends

When I Think About Myself

When I think about myself,
I almost laugh myself to death,
My life has been one great big joke,
A dance that's walked
A song that's spoke,
I laugh so hard I almost choke
When I think about myself.

Sixty years in these folks' world
The child I works for calls me girl
I say "Yes ma'am" for working's sake.
Too proud to bend
Too poor to break,
I laugh until my stomach ache,
When I think about myself.

My folks can make me split my side,
I laughed so hard I nearly died,
The tales they tell, sound just like lying,
They grow the fruit,
But eat the rind,
I laugh until I start to crying,
When I think about my folks.

On a Bright Day, Next Week

On a bright day, next week
Just before the bomb falls
Just before the world ends,
    Just before I die

All my tears will powder
Black in dust like ashes
Black like Buddha's belly
    Black and hot and dry

Then will mercy tumble
Falling down in godheads
Falling on the children
    Falling from the sky

Letter to an Aspiring Junkie

Let me hip you to the streets,
Jim,
Ain't nothing happening.
Maybe some tomorrows gone up in smoke,
raggedy preachers, telling a joke
to lonely, son-less old ladies' maids.

Nothing happening,
Nothing shakin', Jim.
A slough of young cats riding that
cold, white horse,
a grey old monkey on their back, of course
does rodeo tricks.

No haps, man.
No haps.
A worn-out pimp, with a space-age conk,
setting up some fool for a game of tonk,
or poker or
get 'em dead and alive.

The streets?
Climb into the streets man, like you climb
into the ass end of a lion.
Then it's fine.
It's a bug-a-loo and a shing-a-ling,
African dreams on a buck-and-a-wing and a prayer.
That's the streets man,
Nothing happening.

Miss Scarlett, Mr. Rhett
and Other Latter-Day Saints

Novitiates sing Ave
Before the whipping posts,
Criss-crossing their breasts and
tear-stained robes
in the yielding dark.

Animated by the human sacrifice
(Golgotha in black-face)
Priests glow purely white on the
bar-relief of a plantation shrine.

(O Sing)
You are gone but not forgotten
Hail, Scarlett. Requiescat in pace.

God-Makers smear brushes in
blood/gall
to etch frescoes on your
ceilinged tomb.

(O Sing)
Hosanna, King Kotton.

Shadowed couplings of infidels
tempt stigmata from the nipples
of your true-believers.

(Chant Maternoster)
Hallowed Little Eva.

Ministers make novena with the
charred bones of four
very small
very black
very young children

(Intone D I X I E)

And guard the relics
of your intact hymen
daily putting to death,
into eternity,
The stud, his seed,
His seed
His seed.

(O Sing)
Hallelujah, pure Scarlett
Blessed Rhett, the Martyr.

Times-Square-Shoeshine-Composition

I'm the best that ever done it
(pow pow)
     that's my title and I won it
     (pow pow)
I ain't lying, I'm the best
(pow pow)
     Come and put me to the test
     (pow pow)

I'll clean 'em til they squeak
(pow pow)
     In the middle of next week,
     (pow pow)
I'll shine 'em til they whine
(pow pow)
     Till they call me master mine
     (pow pow)

For a quarter and a dime
(pow pow)
     You can get the dee luxe shine
     (pow pow)
Say you wanta pay a quarter?
(pow pow)
     Then you give that to your daughter
     (pow pow)

I ain't playing dozens mister
(pow pow)
    You can give it to your sister
    (pow pow)
Any way you want to read it
(pow pow)
    Maybe it's your momma need it.
    (pow pow)

Say I'm like a greedy bigot,
(pow pow)
    I'm a cap'tilist, can you dig it?
    (pow pow)

Faces

Faces and more remember
then reject
the brown caramel days of youth
Reject the sun-sucked tit of
childhood mornings.
Poke a muzzle of war in the trust frozen eyes
                                            of a favored doll
Breathe, Brother
and displace a moment's hate with organized love.
A poet screams "CHRIST WAITS AT THE SUBWAY!"
But who sees?

To a Freedom Fighter

You drink a bitter draught.
I sip the tears your eyes fight to hold
A cup of lees, of henbane steeped in chaff.
Your breast is hot,
Your anger black and cold,
Through evening's rest, you dream
I hear the moans, you die a thousands' death.
When cane straps flog the body
dark and lean, you feel the blow,
I hear it in your breath.

Riot: 6o's

Our
YOUR FRIEND CHARLIE pawnshop
was a glorious blaze
I heard the flames lick
then eat the trays
of zircons
mounted in red gold alloys

Easter clothes and stolen furs
burned in the attic
radios and teevees
crackled with static
plugged in
only to a racial outlet

Some
thought the FRIENDLY FINANCE FURNITURE CO.
burned higher
When a leopard print sofa with gold legs
(which makes into a bed)
caught fire
an admiring groan from the waiting horde
"Absentee landlord
you got that shit"

Lighting: a hundred Watts
Detroit, Newark and New York
Screeching nerves, exploding minds
lives tied to
a policeman's whistle
a welfare worker's doorbell
finger.

Hospitality, southern-style
corn pone grits and you-all smile
whole blocks novae
brand new stars
policemen caught in their
brand new cars
Chugga chugga chigga
git me one nigga
lootin' n burnin'
he wont git far

Watermelons, summer ripe
grey neck bones and boiling tripe
supermarket roastin like the
noon-day sun
national guard nervous with his shiny gun
goose the motor quicker
here's my nigga picka
shoot him in the belly
shoot him while he run.

We Saw Beyond Our Seeming

We saw beyond our seeming
    These days of bloodied screaming

Of children dying bloated
    Out where the lilies floated

Of men all noosed and dangling
    Within the temples strangling

Our guilt   grey fungus growing
    We knew and lied our knowing

Deafened and unwilling
    We aided in the killing

And now our souls lie broken
    Dry tablets without token.

Black Ode

Your beauty is a thunder
and I am set a wandering—a wandering
Deafened
Down twilight tin-can alleys
And moist sounds
"OOo wee Baby, Look what you could get if your name
                                    was Willie"

Oh, to dip your words like snuff.

A laughter, black and streaming
And I am come a being—a being
Rounded
Up Baptist, aisles, so moaning
And moist sounds
"Bless her heart. Take your bed and walk.
                        You been heavy burdened"
Oh, to lick your love like tears.

No No No No

No
the two legg'd beasts
that walk like men
play stink finger in their crusty asses
while crackling babies
in napalm coats
stretch mouths to receive
burning tears
on splitting tongues
JUST GIVE ME A COOL DRINK OF WATER 'FORE I DIIIE

No
the gap legg'd whore
of the eastern shore
enticing Europe to COME
in her
and turns her pigeon shit back to me
to me
Who stoked the coal that drove the ships
which brought her over the sinuous cemetery
Of my many brothers

No
the cocktailed after noons
of what can I do.
In my white layed pink world
I've let your men cram my mouth
with their black throbbing hate
and I swallowed after
I've let your mammies
steal from my kitchens
(I was always half-amused)
I've chuckled the chins of
your topsy-haired pickaninnies.
What more can I do?
I'll never be black like you.
(HALLELUJAH)

No
the red-shoed priests riding
palanquined
in barefoot children country.
the plastered saints gazing down
beneficently
on kneeling mothers
picking undigested beans
from yesterday's shit.

I have waited
toes curled, hat rolled
heart and genitals
in hand
on the back porches
of forever
in the kitchens and fields
of rejections
on the cold marble steps
of America's White Out-House
in the drop seats of buses
and the open flies of war

No more
the dream that you
will cease haunting me
down in fetid swamps of fear
and will turn to embrace your own
humanity
which I AM

No more
The hope that
the razored insults
which mercury slide over your tongue
will be forgotten
and you will learn the words of love
Mother Brother Father Sister Lover Friend

My hopes
dying slowly
rose petals falling
beneath an autumn red moon
will not adorn your unmarked graves

My dreams
lying quietly
a dark pool under the trees
will not carry your name
to a forgetful shore
And what a pity

What a pity
That pity has folded in upon itself
an old man's mouth
whose teeth are gone
and I have no pity.

My Guilt

My guilt is "slavery's chains," too long
the clang of iron falls down the years.
This brother's sold. This sister's gone
is bitter wax, lining my ears.
My guilt made music with the tears.

My crime is "heroes, dead and gone"
dead Vesey, Turner, Gabriel,
dead Malcolm, Marcus, Martin King.
They fought too hard, they loved too well.
My crime is I'm alive to tell.

My sin is "hanging from a tree"
I do not scream, it makes me proud.
I take to dying like a man.
I do it to impress the crowd.
My sin lies in not screaming loud.

The Calling of Names

He went to being called a Colored man
after answering to "hey nigger,"
Now that's a big jump,
anyway you figger,
     Hey, Baby, Watch my smoke.
From colored man to Negro
With the N in caps,
was like saying Japanese
instead of saying Japs.
     I mean, during the war.
The next big step
was a change for true,
From Negro in caps
to being a Jew.
     Now, Sing Yiddish Mama.
Light, Yellow, Brown
and Dark brown skin,
were o.k. colors to
describe him then,
     He was a Bouquet of Roses.
He changed his seasons
like an almanac,
Now you'll get hurt
if you don't call him "Black."
     Nigguh, I ain't playin' this time.

On Working White Liberals

I don't ask the Foreign Legion
Or anyone to win my freedom
Or to fight my battle better than I can,

Though there's one thing that I cry for
I believe enough to die for
That is every man's responsibility to man.

I'm afraid they'll have to prove first
that they'll watch the Black man move first
Then follow him with faith to kingdom come,
This rocky road is not paved for us,
So, I'll believe in Liberal's aid for us
When I see a white man load a Black man's gun.

Sepia Fashion Show

Their hair, pomaded, faces jaded
bones protruding, hip-wise,
The models strutted, backed and butted,
Then stuck their mouths out, lip-wise.

They'd nasty manners, held like banners,
while they looked down their nose-wise,
I'd see 'em in hell, before they'd sell
me one thing they're wearing, clothes-wise.

The Black Bourgeois, who all say "yah"
When yeah is what they're meaning
Should look around, both up and down
before they set out preening.

"Indeed" they swear, "that's what I'll wear
When I go country-clubbing,"
I'd remind them please, look at those knees
you got a Miss Ann's scrubbing.

The Thirteens (Black)

Your Momma took to shouting
Your Poppa's gone to war,
Your sister's in the streets
Your brother's in the bar,
The thirteens. Right On.

Your cousin's taking smack
Your Uncle's in the joint,
Your buddy's in the gutter
Shooting for his point
The thirteens. Right on.

And you, you make me sorry
You out here by yourself,
I'd call you something dirty,
But there just ain't nothing left,
cept
The thirteens. Right On.

The Thirteens (White)

Your Momma kissed the chauffeur,
Your Poppa balled the cook,
Your sister did the dirty,
in the middle of the book,
The thirteens. Right On.

Your daughter wears a jock strap,
Your son he wears a bra
Your brother jonesed your cousin
in the back seat of the car.
The thirteens. Right On.

Your money thinks you're something
But if I'd learned to curse,
I'd tell you what your name is
But there just ain't nothing worse
than
The thirteens. Right On.

Harlem Hopscotch

One foot down, then hop! It's hot.
    Good things for the ones that's got.
Another jump, now to the left.
    Everybody for hisself.

In the air, now both feet down.
    Since you black, don't stick around.
Food is gone, the rent is due,
    Curse and cry and then jump two.

All the people out of work,
    Hold for three, then twist and jerk.
Cross the line, they count you out.
    That's what hopping's all about.

Both feet flat, the game is done.
They think I lost. I think I won.

Oh Pray
My Wings
Are Gonna
Fit Me Well

To PAUL

Pickin Em Up
and Layin Em Down

There's a long-legged girl
in San Francisco
by the Golden Gate.
She said she'd give me all I wanted
but I just couldn't wait.
I started to
Pickin em up
   and layin em down,
Pickin em up
   and layin em down,
Pickin em up
   and layin em down,
gettin to the next town
Baby.

There's a pretty brown
in Birmingham
Boys, she little and cute
but when she like to tied me down
I had to grab my suit and started to
Pickin em up
   and layin em down,
Pickin em up
   and layin em down,

Pickin em up
                    and layin em down,
gettin to the next town
Baby.

I met that lovely Detroit lady
and thought my time had come
But just before I said "I do"
I said "I got to run" and started to
Pickin em up
                    and layin em down,
Pickin em up
                    and layin em down,
Pickin em up
                    and layin em down,
gettin to the next town
Baby.

There ain't no words for what I feel
about a pretty face
But if I stay I just might miss
a prettier one some place
I started to
Pickin em up
                    and layin em down,
Pickin em up
                    and layin em down,
Pickin em up
                    and layin em down,
gettin to the next town
Baby.

Here's to Adhering

I went to a party
    out in Hollywood,
The atmosphere was shoddy
    but the drinks were good,
        and that's where I heard you laugh.

I then went cruising
    on an old Greek ship,
The crew was amusing
    but the guests weren't hip,
        that's where I found your hands.

On to the Sahara
    in a caravan,
The sun struck like an arrow
    but the nights were grand,
        and that's how I found your chest.

An evening in the Congo
    where the Congo ends,
I found myself alone, oh
    but I made some friends,
        that's where I saw your face.

I have been devoting
    all my time to get

Parts of you out floating
　　　still unglued as yet.

Won't you pull yourself together

For

　　　Me

　　O N C E

On Reaching Forty

Other acquainted years
sidle
with modest
decorum
across the scrim of toughened
tears and to a stage
planked with laughter boards
and waxed with rueful loss
But forty
with the authorized
brazenness of a uniformed
cop stomps
no-knocking
into the script
bumps a funky grind on the
shabby curtain of youth
and delays the action.

Unless you have the inborn
wisdom
and grace
and are clever enough
to die at
thirty-nine.

The Telephone

It comes in black
and blue, indecisive
beige. In red and chaperons my life.
Sitting like a strict
and spinstered Aunt
spiked between my needs
and need.

It tats the day, crocheting
other people's lives
in neat arrangements
ignoring me
busy with the hemming
of strangers' overlong affairs or
the darning of my
neighbors' worn-out
dreams.

From Monday, the morning of the week,
through mid-times
noon and Sunday's dying
light. It sits silent.
Its needle sound
does not transfix my ear
or draw my longing to
a close.

Ring. Damn you!

Part Two

Passing Time

Your skin like dawn
Mine like dusk.

One paints the beginning
of a certain end.

The other, the end of a
sure beginning.

Now Long Ago

One innocent spring
your voice meant to me
less than tires turning
on a distant street.

Your name, perhaps spoken,
led no chorus of
batons
unrehearsed
to crush against my
empty chest.

That cool spring
was shortened by
your summer, bold impatient
and all forgotten
except when silence
turns the key
into my midnight bedroom
and comes to sleep upon your
pillow.

Greyday

The day hangs heavy
loose and grey
when you're away.

A crown of thorns
a shirt of hair
is what I wear.

No one knows
my lonely heart
when we're apart.

Poor Girl

You've got another love
    and I know it
Someone who adores you
    just like me
Hanging on your words
    like they were gold
Thinking that she understands
    your soul
Poor Girl
      Just like me.

You're breaking another heart
    and I know it
And there's nothing
    I can do
If I try to tell her
    what I know
She'll misunderstand
    and make me go
Poor Girl
      Just like me.

You're going to leave her too
    and I know it
She'll never know
    what made you go

She'll cry and wonder
    what went wrong
Then she'll begin
    to sing this song
Poor Girl
      Just like me.

Come. And Be My Baby

The highway is full of big cars
going nowhere fast
And folks is smoking anything that'll burn
Some people wrap their lives around a cocktail glass
And you sit wondering
where you're going to turn
I got it.
Come. And be my baby.

Some prophets say the world is gonna end tomorrow
But others say we've got a week or two
The paper is full of every kind of blooming horror
And you sit wondering
What you're gonna do.
I got it.
Come. And be my baby.

Senses of Insecurity

I couldn't tell fact from fiction
    or if my dream was true,
The only sure prediction
    in this whole world was you.
I'd touched your features inchly
    heard love and dared the cost.
The scented spiel reeled me unreal
    and found my senses lost.

Alone

Lying, thinking
Last night
How to find my soul a home
Where water is not thirsty
And bread loaf is not stone
I came up with one thing
And I don't believe I'm wrong
That nobody,
But nobody
Can make it out here alone.

Alone, all alone
Nobody, but nobody
Can make it out here alone.

There are some millionaires
With money they can't use
Their wives run round like banshees
Their children sing the blues
They've got expensive doctors
To cure their hearts of stone.
But nobody
No nobody
Can make it out here alone.

Alone, all alone
Nobody, but nobody
Can make it out here alone.

Now if you listen closely
I'll tell you what I know
Storm clouds are gathering
The wind is gonna blow
The race of man is suffering
And I can hear the moan,
Cause nobody,
But nobody
Can make it out here alone.

Alone, all alone
Nobody, but nobody
Can make it out here alone.

Communication I

She wished of him a lover's kiss and
nights of coupled twining
They laced themselves
between the trees
and to the water's edge.

Reminding her
the cratered moon lay light years away
he spoke of Greece, the Parthenon
and Cleopatra's barge.

She splayed her foot
up to the shin
within the ocean brine.

He quoted Pope and Bernard Shaw
and Catcher in the Rye.

Her sandal lost
she dried her toe
and then she mopped her brow.

Dry-eyed
she walked into her room
and frankly told her mother
"Of all he said I understood,
he said he loved another."

For Adele

Communication II

The Student

Thc dust of ancient pages
had never touched his face,
and fountains black and comely
were mummyied in a place
beyond
his young un-knowing.

The Teacher

She shared the lettered strivings
of etched Pharaonic walls
and Reconstruction's anguish
resounded down the halls
of all her
dry dreams.

Wonder

A day
drunk with the nectar of
nowness
weaves its way between
the years
to find itself at the flophouse
of night
to sleep and be seen
no more.

Will I be less
dead because I wrote this
poem or you more because
you read it
long years hence.

A Conceit

Give me your hand

Make room for me
to lead and follow
you
beyond this rage of poetry.

Let others have
the privacy of
touching words
and love of loss
of love.

For me
Give me your hand.

Part Three

Request

If this country is a bastard
will the lowdown mother user
who ran off
and left the woman
moaning in her
green delivery
please come back and claim
his love child.
Give a legal name to beg from
for the first
time of its life.

Africa

Thus she had lain
sugar cane sweet
deserts her hair
golden her feet
mountains her breasts
two Niles her tears
Thus she has lain
Black through the years.

Over the white seas
rime white and cold
brigands ungentled
icicle bold
took her young daughters
sold her strong sons
churched her with Jesus
bled her with guns.
Thus she has lain.

Now she is rising
remember her pain
remember the losses
her screams loud and vain
remember her riches
her history slain
now she is striding
although she had lain.

America

The gold of her promise
    has never been mined

Her borders of justice
    not clearly defined

Her crops of abundance
    the fruit and the grain

Have not fed the hungry
    nor eased that deep pain

Her proud declarations
    are leaves on the wind

Her southern exposure
    black death did befriend

Discover this country
    dead centuries cry

Erect noble tablets
    where none can decry

"She kills her bright future
    and rapes for a sou

Then entraps her children
    with legends untrue"

I beg you

Discover this country.

For Us, Who Dare Not Dare

Be me a Pharaoh
Build me high pyramids of stone and question
See me the Nile
at twilight
and jaguars moving to
the slow cool draught.

Swim me Congo
Hear me the tails of alligators
flapping waves that reach
a yester shore.

Swing me vines, beyond that Bao-Bab tree,
and talk me chief
Sing me birds
flash color lightening through bright green leaves.

Taste me fruit
its juice free falling from
a mother tree.

Know me

Africa.

for Countee Cullen

Lord, In My Heart

Holy haloes
    Ring me round

Spirit waves on
    Spirit sound

Meshach and
    Abednego

Golden chariot
    Swinging low

I recite them
    in my sleep

Jordan's cold
    and briny deep

Bible lessons
    Sunday school

Bow before the
    Golden Rule

Now I wonder
    If I tried

Could I turn my
    cheek aside

Marvelling with
    afterthought

Let the blow fall
    saying naught

Of my true Christ-
    like control

and the nature
    of my soul.

Would I strike with
    rage divine

Till the culprit
    fell supine

Hit out broad all
    fury red

Till my foes are
    fallen dead

Teachers of my
    early youth

Taught forgiveness
    stressed the truth

Here then is my
    Christian lack:

If I'm struck then
    I'll strike back.

Artful Pose

Of falling leaves and melting
snows, of birds
in their delights
Some poets sing
their melodies
tendering my nights
sweetly.

My pencil halts
and will not go
along that quiet path
I need to write
of lovers false

and hate
and hateful wrath
quickly.

Part Four

The Couple

Discard the fear and what
was she?   of rag and bones
a mimicry of woman's
fairy ness
Archaic at its birth

Discharge the hate and when
was he?   disheveled moans
a mimesis of man's
estate
deceited for its worth

Dissolve the greed and why
were they?   enfeebled thrones
a memory of mortal
kindliness
exiled from this earth.

The Pusher

He bad
O he bad
He make a honky
poot. Make a honky's
blue eyes squint
anus tight, when
my man look in
the light blue eyes.

He thinks
He don't play
His Afro crown raises
eyes. Raises eyebrows
of wonder and dark
envy when he, combed
out, hits the street.

He sleek
Dashiki
Wax printed on his skin
remembrances of Congo dawns
laced across his chest.
Red Blood Red and Black.

He bought
O He got

Malcolm's paper
back. Checked out the
photo, caught a few godly
lines. Then wondered how
many wives/daughters of
Honky (miscalled The Man)
bird snake
caught, dug them both.
(Him, Fro-ed Dashiki-ed
and the book.)

He stashed
He stands stashed
Near, too near the MLK
Library. P.S. naught
naught naught. Breathing
slaughter on the Malcolm X
Institute. Whole fist
balled, fingers pressing
palm. Shooting up through
Honky's blue-eyed sky.

   "BLACK IS!"
   "NATION TIME!"
   "TOMORROW'S GLORY HERE TODAY"

Pry free the hand
Observe our Black present.
There lie soft on that
copper palm, a death of

coke. A kill of horse
eternal night's barbiturates.
One hundred youths
sped down to
Speed.

He right
O he bad
He badder than death
yet gives no sweet
release.

Chicken-Licken

She was afraid of men,
sin and the humors
of the night.
When she saw a bed
locks clicked
in her brain.

She screwed a frown
around and plugged
it in the keyhole.
Put a chain across
her door and closed
her mind.

Her bones were found
round thirty years later
when they razed
her building to
put up a parking lot.

Autopsy: read
dead of acute peoplelessness.

Part Five

I Almost Remember

I almost remember
    smiling some
years past
    even combing the ceiling
with the teeth of a laugh
(longer ago than the
        smile).
Open night news-eyed I watch
channels of hunger
    written on children's faces
    bursting bellies balloon
in the air of my day room.

There was a smile, I recall
now jelled in
a never yester glow. Even a laugh
that tickled the tits of
heaven
(older than the smile).
In graphs, afraid, I see the black
brown hands and
white thin yellowed fingers.

Slip slipping from the
ledge of life. Forgotten by
all but hatred.

Ignored
by all but disdain.

On late evenings when
quiet inhabits my garden
when grass sleeps and
streets are only paths for silent
mist.

I seem to remember

Smiling.

Prisoner

Even sunlight dares
and trembles through
my bars
to shimmer
dances on
the floor.
A clang of
lock and
keys and heels
and blood-dried
guns.
Even sunshine
dares.

It's jail
        and bail
then rails to run.

Guard grey men
serve plates of rattle
noise and concrete
death and beans
Then pale sun stumbles
through the poles of
iron to warm the horror
of grey guard men.

It's jail
        and bail
then rails to run.

Black night. The me
myself of me sleeks
in the folds and history
of fear. To secret hold
me deep and close my
ears of lulls and clangs
and memory of hate.
Then night and sleep
and dreams.

It's jail
        and bail
then rails to run.

Woman Me

Your smile, delicate
rumor of peace.
Deafening revolutions nestle in the
cleavage of
your breasts
Beggar-Kings and red-ringed Priests
seek glory at the meeting
of your thighs
A grasp of Lions,   A lap of Lambs.

    Your tears, jeweled
    strewn a diadem
    caused Pharaohs to ride
    deep in the bosom of the
    Nile. Southern spas lash fast
    their doors upon the night when
    winds of death blow down your name
    A bride of hurricanes,   A swarm of summer wind.

Your laughter, pealing tall
above the bells of ruined cathedrals.
Children reach between your teeth
for charts to live their lives.
A stomp of feet,   A bevy of swift hands.

John J.

His soul curdled
standing milk
          childhood's right gone wrong.

Plum blue, skin brown dusted
eyes black shining,
           (His momma didn't want him)

The round head slick silk
Turn around, fall down curls
Old ladies smelling of flour
and talcum powder Cashmere Bouquet, said
"This child is pretty enough to be a girl."
           (But his momma didn't want him)

John J. grinned a "How can you resist me?"
and danced to conjure lightning from
a morning's summer sky.
Gave the teacher an apple kiss
           (But his momma didn't want him)

His nerves stretched two thousand miles
found a flinging singing lady,
breasting a bar
calling straights on the dice,
gin over ice,

and the 30's version of
everybody in the
pool.

(She didn't want him.)

Southeast Arkanasia

After Eli Whitney's gin
brought to generations' end
bartered flesh and broken bones
Did it cleanse you of your sin
     Did you ponder?

Now, when farmers bury wheat
and the cow men dump the sweet
butter down on Davy Jones
Does it sanctify your street
       Do you wonder?

Or is guilt your nightly mare
bucking wake your evenings' share
of the stilled repair of groans
and the absence of despair
        over yonder?

Song for the Old Ones

My Fathers sit on benches
    their flesh count every plank
    the slats leave dents of darkness
deep in their withered flanks.

They nod like broken candles
    all waxed and burnt profound,
    they say "It's understanding
that makes the world go round."

There in those pleated faces
    I see the auction block
    the chains and slavery's coffles
the whip and lash and stock.

My Fathers speak in voices
    that shred my fact and sound
    they say "It's our submission
that makes the world go round."

They used the finest cunning
    their naked wits and wiles
    the lowly Uncle Tomming
and Aunt Jemimas' smiles.

They've laughed to shield their crying
     then shuffled through their dreams
     and stepped 'n fetched a country
to write the blues with screams.

I understand their meaning
     it could and did derive
     from living on the edge of death
They kept my race alive.

Child Dead in Old Seas

Father,
I wait for you in oceans
tides washing pyramids high
above my head.
Waves, undulating
corn rows around my
black feet.
The heavens shift and
stars find holes set
new in dark infirmity.
My search goes on.
Dainty shells on ash-like wrists
of debutantes remember you.
Childhood's absence has
not stilled your
voice. My ear
listens. You whisper
on the watery passage.

Deep dirges moan
from the
belly of the sea
and your song
floats to me
of lost savannahs
green and

drums. Of palm trees bending
woman-like swaying
grape-blue children
laugh on beaches
of sand as
white as your bones
clean
on the foot of
long-ago waters.

Father.
I wait for you
wrapped in
the entrails of
whales. Your
blood now
blues
spume
over
the rippled
surface of our
grave.

Take Time Out

When you see them
on a freeway hitching rides
wearing beads
with packs by their sides
you ought to ask
What's all the
warring and the jarring
and the
killing and
the thrilling
all about.

Take Time Out.

When you see him
with a band around his head
and an army surplus bunk
that makes his bed. You'd
better ask What's
all the
beating and
the cheating and
the bleeding and
the needing
all about.

Take Time Out.

When you see her walking
Barefoot in the rain
And you know she's tripping
on a one-way train
you need to ask
what's all the
lying and the
dying and
the running and
the gunning
all about.

Take Time Out.

Use a minute
feel some sorrow
for the folks
who think tomorrow
is a place that they
can call up
on the phone.
Take a month
and show some kindness
for the folks
who thought that blindness
was an illness that
affected eyes alone.

If you know that youth
is dying on the run

and my daughter trades
dope stories with your son
we'd better see
what all our
fearing and our
jeering and our
crying and
our lying
brought about.

Take Time Out.

for Harriet Tubman & Fredrick Douglass

Elegy

I lay down in my grave
and watch my children
grow
Proud blooms
above the weeds of death.

Their petals wave
and still nobody
knows the soft black
dirt that is my winding
sheet. The worms, my friends,
yet tunnel holes in
bones and through those
apertures I see the rain.
The sunfelt warmth
now jabs
within my space and
brings me roots of my
children born.

Their seeds must fall
and press beneath
this earth,
and find me where I

wait. My only need to
fertilize their birth.

I lay down in my grave
and watch my children
grow.

Reverses

How often must we
  butt to head
Mind to ass
  flank to nuts
  cock to elbow
  hip to toe
  soul to shoulder
  confront ourselves
  in our past.

Little Girl Speakings

Ain't nobody better's my Daddy,
     you keep yo' quauter
     I ain't yo' daughter,
Ain't nobody better's my Daddy.

Ain't nothing prettier'n my dollie
     heard what I said,
     don't pat her head,
Ain't nothing prettier'n my dollie.

No lady cookinger than my Mommy
     smell that pie,
     see I don't lie
No lady cookinger than my Mommy.

This Winter Day

The kitchen is its readiness
white green and orange things
leak their blood selves in the soup.

Ritual sacrifice that snaps
an odor at my nose and starts
my tongue to march
slipping in the liquid of it drip.

The day, silver striped
in rain, is balked against
my window and the soup.